BE CAREFUL!
TURTLES AHEAD

by Maya Arora
illustrated by Kathie Kelleher

Orlando   Boston   Dallas   Chicago   San Diego

Visit *The Learning Site!*

www.harcourtschool.com

Sea turtles have lived on Earth for a long time. They spend most of their lives in the ocean. However, they hatch from eggs in nests dug in the sand. These nests are on beaches, such as Long Beach, North Carolina.

Long Beach is an important place for sea turtles. They need a clean place to lay their eggs. Without beaches like this, sea turtles cannot survive.

3

Turtles that come to Long Beach to lay their eggs may remember this place. It is where they once hatched. Sea turtles can live a hundred years. The last time they were here, there may not have been as many people.

People who come to Long Beach may not know about sea turtles. They may harm them and not know it. To protect the turtles, a group of Long Beach adults and kids have formed a turtle patrol.

5

This patrol helps the turtle eggs survive until they hatch. Its members are trained to look for signs that sea turtles have been on the beach. A sea turtle's tracks are a sign that the turtle has come to make her nest.

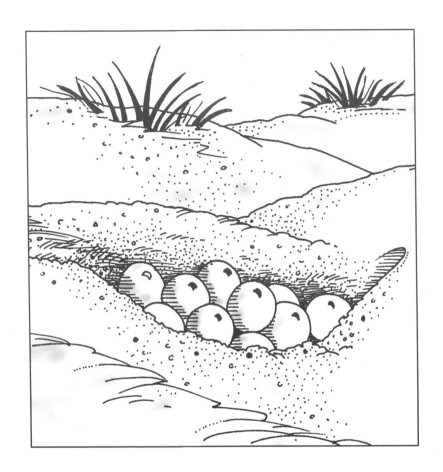

Sea turtles build their nests at night because it is safer. A female turtle will creep up the beach and look patiently for the right spot. Then she begins to dig with her flippers. It takes her about half an hour to dig the hole.

Once she has dug the hole that will be the nest, the turtle lays about one hundred eggs the size of table tennis balls. The shells look and feel like leather. They are soft and will not break. Then the sea turtle covers the hole and returns to the ocean.

In the morning, the people on patrol find turtle tracks. These tracks lead them to a new nest. They put up a sign that says, "Do Not Disturb. A Sea Turtle Nest Is Here." This message will warn people to stay away from the nest.

9

Every day, people on patrol look for new nests. They make sure other nests are still safe. They also clean litter off the beach and make sure that the warning signs are still up.

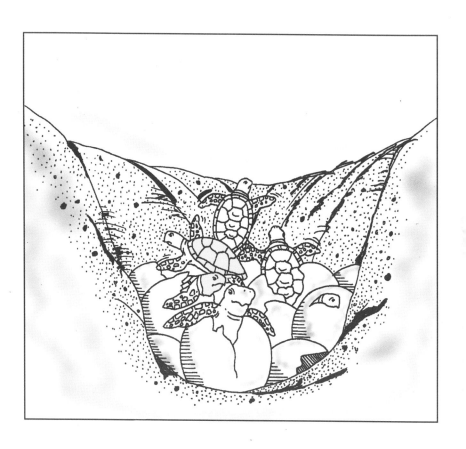

After about two months, it is time
for the eggs to hatch. The eggs hatch at
night. Each baby turtle has a sharp
tooth called an egg tooth. The baby
uses this tooth to rip open its shell.
The new turtles are about the size of a
half dollar.

11

It takes a couple of days for the babies to dig out of the nest and get to the surface of the beach.

During this time, the patrol keeps people away from the nest. The people at the beach are eager to watch, and they often get too close. The baby turtles must be left alone.

The baby turtles leave their nest at night. They look for the place with the most light. Because it is dark, the ocean and sky have the most light. A patrol member may shine a flashlight at the shore to help turtles find the water.

13

The babies have to hurry, though.
This is the most dangerous time of
their lives. The tiny turtles are easily
eaten by predators, such as raccoons
and crabs.

   With the help of the patrol, the tiny
turtles make it to the sea. They swim
nearby for a day, and then they
disappear. No one is sure what happens
to them.

15

In about twenty years, the female turtles come back. They are now wise adults. They return to this very beach, where they once hatched, to lay their own eggs in the sand.